C000050458

Ministering Communion

by
Fr Allen Morris

*All booklets are published thanks to the
generous support of the members of the
Catholic Truth Society*

CATHOLIC TRUTH SOCIETY
PUBLISHERS TO THE HOLY SEE

Contents

All rights reserved. First published 2015 by The Incorporated Catholic Truth Society, 40-46 Harleyford Road London SE11 5AY Tel: 020 7640 0042 Fax: 020 7640 0046. © 2015 The Incorporated Catholic Truth Society.

ISBN 978 1 78469 041 0

Liturgical Ministry: What is Liturgy?
What is Ministry?

Liturgy is the public worship of the Church. It is first and foremost a participation in Christ's worship of the Father, and it is in this worship that the Church is most evidently herself.

Christ is always present in his Church, especially in her liturgical celebrations. He is present in the sacrifice of the Mass, not only in the person of his minister, "the same now offering, through the ministry of priests, who formerly offered himself on the cross", but especially under the eucharistic species. By his power he is present in the sacraments, so that when a man baptizes it is really Christ himself who baptizes. He is present in his word, since it is he himself who speaks when the holy Scriptures are read in the Church. He is present, lastly, when the Church prays and sings, for He promised: "Where two or three are gathered together in my name, there am I in the midst of them" (*Mt* 18:20).

Christ indeed always associates the Church with Himself in this great work wherein God is perfectly glorified and men are sanctified. The Church is his beloved Bride who calls to her Lord, and through him offers worship to the Eternal Father.

Rightly, then, the liturgy is considered as an exercise of the priestly office of Jesus Christ. In the liturgy the sanctification of the man is signified by signs perceptible to the senses, and is effected in a way which corresponds with each of these signs; in the liturgy the whole public worship is performed by the Mystical Body of Jesus Christ, that is, by the Head and his members.

From this it follows that every liturgical celebration, because it is an action of Christ the priest and of his Body which is the Church, is a sacred action surpassing all others; no other action of the Church can equal its efficacy by the same title and to the same degree.

The liturgy is the summit toward which the activity of the Church is directed; at the same time it is the font from which all her power flows. For the aim and object of apostolic works is that all who are made sons of God by faith and baptism should come together to praise God in the midst of his Church, to take part in the sacrifice, and to eat the Lord's supper.

Sacrosanctum Concilium 7, 10

Liturgy is always something more than just what we happen to do in this place, here and now. It is always a work of the whole Church. It is most fundamentally the participation of the whole Church, the Body of Christ, in the worship offered to God the Father by God the Son, Jesus Christ. It is a work that is visible here on earth but which is, invisible to us, shared in also by saints and angels.

The ordinary forms of the Liturgy are those contained in the Church's ritual books. The most regularly celebrated are the Liturgy of the Hours and the Mass, but also included are the rites of Baptism, Confirmation, Penance, Marriage etc (the Sacraments), the rites of Christian Funerals, and rites of Blessing.

Liturgy is always intended to be prayerful, drawing us into the prayer and worship of Jesus Christ. But not all prayer is liturgical prayer. Our private prayers – such as *lectio divina* or the Rosary, or our quiet personal prayer – have a different character. Even when they are spiritual exercises especially commended by the Church they are private prayers. Prayer of this sort helps deepen our relationship with God and helps us better live our Christian lives. However in this prayer we pray essentially as individuals who come before God in our own right, and set before him ourselves, our needs, our hopes and fears. This is the case even when we pray such forms of prayer together with others, even in church.

Liturgy always has the broader ecclesial dimension, and always it is a participation in the prayer of Christ.

For this reason the Church takes the greatest care of how the Liturgy is celebrated. The liturgical books themselves

witness to the care taken with regard to the proper ordering
of the rites. There is clear instruction about what is to be
done, at Mass for example.[1] The roles of the ministers and
the congregation as a whole are described. The approved
readings and prayers are provided. There is guidance about
the way symbols are used and how the church building
itself is to be arranged. Nothing is left to chance! But
of course the guidance has to be applied to particular
celebrations in particular places and at particular times.

Ministry

Christian ministry is a sharing in the mission and ministry
of Jesus Christ. It is a participation made possible by
our baptism, where we are anointed with the chrism of
salvation so that, united with the Church, we may remain,
each of us, for ever members of Christ who is Priest,
Prophet and King.

This ministry which is the duty and right of all the
baptised is carried out in so many ways. Some of these are
the responsibility of those called to particular ministry and
ordained as deacon, priest or bishop so that they may carry
out the work entrusted to them. More usually the ministry
is carried out by laymen and women in the daily business
of family life, at work, and as active citizens of their local,
national and international communities. Whatever the
differences, all Christians are called to be united in making
this world holy, in witnessing to the Gospel of Jesus Christ

by word and deed, and in living the love of God, especially in the service of those most in need.

Mostly Christian ministry is to be exercised in the 'world' in our towns and cities, in our places of work and in our homes – wherever it is that daily life and the mission of the Church takes us. However some part of it is also exercised in church! And of that part, which includes administration, fundraising and a variety of other works, an especially important part is liturgical ministry.

Liturgical Ministry

One of my privileges as a parish priest is introducing children to their first exercise of liturgical ministry. It is usually as they prepare to be altar servers. At the very first training session I ask them who it is that, as servers, they are there to serve. The answers are interesting, and revealing.

Often the first answer is 'God'. I tell them that although that is true, that is not the answer I am looking for.

Then someone will say that they are there to serve me! I tell them that that is also true. And that I am very grateful. But that it is not the answer I am looking for.

Then, usually, someone will give me the answer I hope for: 'We are here to serve everybody else.' And I thank them for that answer – and say that when they do that God and the priest will be very happy, because in the liturgy God and the priest also are there to serve 'everybody else', the congregation, helping them to the full active and conscious participation in the liturgy that, through baptism, is their right and their duty.

Ministries to the Liturgy take a wide variety of forms. In the General Instruction to the Roman Missal (GIRM) there is mention of that of Bishop, Priest and Deacon, called the ordained ministries; the ministry of the congregation (who are also there to serve as well as be served); acolyte and lector[2] (in practice these ministries are reserved for those preparing for ordination); altar servers, commissioned ministers of the word, psalmist, the *schola* or choir, cantor, sacristan, those who take up the collection, those who welcome people to the church, and Master of Ceremonies.[3] One might add to the list those responsible for the preparation of the Liturgy – for example the choosing of settings for the Liturgy's sung parts, and the decoration, even the cleaning, of the church where the Liturgy will be celebrated.

Ordinary and extraordinary

Attentive readers of the preceding paragraph will notice that there is no mention of ministers of Holy Communion. This requires an explanation.

The expectation is that Holy Communion will be distributed by the clergy present – this being an ordinary or integral dimension of their ministry. Where there are not sufficient ordinary ministers present for the distribution of Holy Communion in a timely and appropriate manner, 'extraordinary' ministers can be called on to assist. They are described as extraordinary (sometimes as 'special' ministers) simply because they are not the 'ordinary' ministers.

However, because in English we often use the word 'extraordinary' to mean what is more important than 'ordinary' (which would be misleading in this particular case) the word 'commissioned' is also used to refer to those lay ministers who assist in the 'ordinary' ministers (the clergy) in the distribution of Holy Communion.[4]

The norms of the Church are that acolytes should be the delegated minister to assist in the distribution of Holy Communion where there are not sufficient ordinary ministers. In practice Bishops have chosen to confer these lay ministries of acolyte and lector only on for those preparing for ordination, as they are only permitted to be conferred on men. Wishing to see both women and men exercise the ministry of proclaiming the readings from sacred Scripture, and (where lay ministers are needed) the distribution of Holy Communion, they have instead not instituted acolytes and lectors in parishes, but instead commissioned 'readers' and 'ministers of Holy Communion' instead.

Collaborative Ministry

The vision of the Church is that the celebration of the Liturgy be seen as a work not only of the ordained minister (essential though that is, for example, the celebration of

Mass and some of the other sacraments) but of the gathered Church. The ministers called from the community, and called in some number according to the above list, are there to assist that community in its praying of the Liturgy.

The ministers draw on their own particular skills and ability to serve the Liturgy, to allow the beauty and dignity and pace appropriate to the Liturgy to communicate itself to the congregation, so that the community gathered may celebrate worthily and fruitfully.

Training is essential for the proper exercise of ministry. Sometimes the ministry will require that the person exercising it will develop exceptional skills – musicians need to have a certain competency in their instrument, singers know how to use their voice, and each group has to rehearse with the other so that the congregation will be helped and not hindered by the resulting sounds. Sometimes the ministry may be less specialised, less demanding but always a ministry can be exercised well or less well. Training helps it to be exercised well.

The minimum training will include ensuring ministers know

- the coordinator for their ministry (not least so they can let someone know if they are on the rota but cannot minister that day for some reason)

- the practicalities for that day (take collectors for example: where are the baskets are kept? Is there a second collection today or not? Or take readers for another example – what are the readings set for a particular day?)

- the safeguarding responsibilities involved (take ministers of hospitality for example: what are the safe places for those in wheelchairs to sit? What is the policy in case of fire or other need for emergency evacuation?)

- with which other ministers they need to coordinate their ministry with (musicians and readers, for example: is the Psalm being sung or said? What is happening with the Gospel Acclamation?)

However the minimum is far from being enough. Ministers need and deserve to understand how their ministry helps to support and build up the community of the Church; why the Liturgy is important and how it helps us to mature as Christians. They need and deserve also to be thanked and encouraged and helped to bond as a particular *cadre* within the family of the parish, and not only so as better to be able to support and encourage each other in the work of being a minister – which often is costly and demanding on people's time. When people are giving as much as our ministers do, they deserve their own time for care and support.

Commissioning of Ministers

The commissioning of ministers is clearly an important moment in the life of a parish, and should take place when a sizeable portion of the parish community is able to be present.

It is better to avoid the great feasts, such as the Mass of the Lord's Supper, as these already have important focusses of their own.

For the commissioning of ministers of Holy Communion, however, the Solemnity of the Most Holy Body and Blood of Christ (Corpus Christi), might be considered, or the parish's feast of the Dedication of the Church.

Local circumstances will suggest whether it is better to commission all ministers at a single celebration, or at the Mass at which they will most regularly serve.

Local circumstances will also determine whether ministers are commissioned for a single year, or for longer.

At the end of their time of service it should be a matter of mutual discernment between minister and parish priest whether they are to be commissioned for a further period of service.

A Theology of the Mass

At the Mass of the Lord's Supper, the first liturgy of the Sacred Paschal Triduum, we hear the following words from St Paul - the first written account of the Eucharist, the Mass, that we possess.

> This is what I received from the Lord, and in turn passed on to you: that on the same night that he was betrayed, the Lord Jesus took some bread, and thanked God for it and broke it, and he said, 'This is my body, which is for you; do this as a memorial of me.' In the same way he took the cup after supper, and said, 'This cup is the new covenant in my blood. Whenever you drink it, do this as a memorial of me.' Until the Lord comes, therefore, every time you eat this bread and drink this cup, you are proclaiming his death.

> 1 *Co* 11:23-26

The passage reminds us of several things.

- The Mass is firmly established in the Paschal Mystery of Jesus's Passion, Death and Resurrection

- The Mass is about the gift of Jesus's body and blood, the new covenant offered to us.

- The Mass is an expression of the Tradition of the Church, handed on through the Church down the ages, and presently entrusted to us.

- Our participation in the Mass - especially in the eating and drinking of the Lord's Body and Blood - is a memorial, an active remembering, of him. And our participation means that we here and now proclaim and witness to our faith in his saving death.

The *Catechism of the Catholic Church* (CCC), quoting the Second Vatican Council's teaching on the Liturgy, puts it this way:

At the Last Supper, on the night he was betrayed, our Saviour instituted the Eucharistic sacrifice of his Body and Blood. This he did in order to perpetuate the sacrifice of the cross throughout the ages until he should come again, and so to entrust to his beloved Spouse, the Church, a memorial of his death and resurrection: a sacrament of love, a sign of unity, a bond of charity, a Paschal banquet 'in which Christ is consumed, the mind is filled with grace, and a pledge of future glory is given to us.'

CCC 1323, quoting *Sacrosanctum Concilium* 47

There is much here to note - including the language of sacrifice, of love and charity, of salvation. These are themes well worth exploring in days of recollection and formation for those who are involved in ministering at celebrations of the Mass.

But here let us note in particular the way in which the passage describes the Mass in terms of a personal work of our Saviour. He institutes the sacrament of the Sacrifice at the Last Supper in anticipation of his offering the sacrifice of himself at the Cross. He does this so that the Church may be present to and given life through that sacrament always, until he comes again. In her reception of this sacrament the Church receives, herself consumes, Christ. She is filled with grace now. And she is encouraged by the pledge of future glory even as she awaits his return in glory. For the Church, by this sacrament, Calvary and the Resurrection are not past events somehow remembered. They are present realities, re-presented to us (re-presented, not merely represented) for Christ wills it. And he wills it for our sake.

The Eucharist is 'the source and summit of the Christian life.' 'The other sacraments, and indeed all ecclesiastical ministries and works of the apostolate, are bound up with the Eucharist and are oriented toward it. For in the blessed Eucharist is contained the whole spiritual good of the Church, namely Christ himself, our Pasch.'

'The Eucharist is the efficacious sign and sublime cause of that communion in the divine life and that unity of the People of God by which the Church is kept in being. It is the culmination both of God's action sanctifying the world in Christ and of the worship men offer to Christ and through him to the Father in the Holy Spirit.'

CCC 1324, 1325

To put all this at its simplest: by the will of Jesus, the
Mass is for us, and we are for the world. Pope Francis
recently said:

> Jesus leaves us the Eucharist as the Church's daily
> remembrance of, and deeper sharing in, the event of
> his Passover (cf. *Lk* 22:19)… The believer is essentially
> 'one who remembers'.
>
> *Evangelii Gaudium*, 13

We cannot remember Jesus, not really remember him,
and not be moved to mission. This is an important point
made by Pope St John Paul II in his letter inaugurating
the 2004-2005 Year of the Eucharist, and it concerns the
authenticity of our communal sharing in the Eucharist:

> In the Eucharist our God has shown love in the extreme,
> overturning all those criteria of power which too often
> govern human relations and radically affirming the
> criterion of service: 'If anyone would be first, he must
> be last of all and servant of all' (*Mc* 9:35). It is not by
> chance that the Gospel of John contains no account of
> the institution of the Eucharist, but instead relates the
> 'washing of feet' (cf. *Jn* 13:1-20): by bending down to
> wash the feet of his disciples, Jesus explains the meaning
> of the Eucharist unequivocally. Saint Paul vigorously
> reaffirms the impropriety of a Eucharistic celebration
> lacking charity expressed by practical sharing with the
> poor (cf. 1 *Co* 11:17-22, 27-34).
>
> *Mane Nobiscum Domine*, 28

The Church uses the language of 'remembering' or of 'memorial' to describe the Eucharist and our participation in it. But it uses the language in a somewhat technical and specialised way.[5] In the ordinary way of things, 'remembering' is something that happens in our mind - the conjuring up of (often rather faded and doubtful) mental memories of some past thing.

The following story - handed on by the Jewish philosopher Martin Buber - demonstrates the power of human memory when it also becomes present reality:

> My grandfather was paralysed. One day he was asked to tell something that happened with his teacher - the great Baalschem. Then he told how the saintly Baalschem used to leap about and dance while he was at his prayers. As he went on with the story my grandfather stood up; he was so carried away that he had to show how the master had done it, and started to caper about and dance. From that moment on he was cured. That is how stories ought to be told.

> Martin Buber, quoted by Michael Mayne,
> *The Enduring Melody*
> (London: Darton, Longman, & Todd, 2006, 204-205).

The transformative power of the Eucharist however does not depend only on the enthusiasm and personal commitment of those Christians present to celebrate. Most importantly it depends on the real presence of Christ. Our new life, gifted to us in the Eucharist, is his present gift. We need to receive it and accept it, and let it take root in us and draw response from us. But first and foremost, through this ritual handed on by the Church, it is Christ himself who is personally and really present to us. It is he who enables our remembering and prompts our response.

The Church knows Christ to be present to us in the Liturgy in many ways.

> Christ is always present in his Church, especially in her liturgical celebrations. He is present in the sacrifice of the Mass, not only in the person of his minister, 'the same now offering, through the ministry of priests, who formerly offered himself on the cross', but especially under the Eucharistic species. By his power he is present in the sacraments, so that when a man baptizes it is really Christ himself who baptizes. He is present in his Word, since it is he himself who speaks when the holy Scriptures are read in the Church. He is present, lastly, when the Church prays and sings, for he promised: 'Where two or three are gathered together in my name, there am I in the midst of them' (*Mt* 18:20).

Sacrosanctum Concilium 7

This is extraordinary. It is a grace of the Paschal Mystery. It is the truth that enables all Liturgy to be the occasion of a new personal encounter between the risen Lord and the community of disciples: an encounter as real as those of which we read in the Gospels - and including in it just the same encouragement and challenge.

The presences of Christ in the various stages of the Mass

The Liturgy of the Mass helps us attend to different presences of the Lord in sequence.

The Introductory Rites engage us with the assembly of the Church in this place at this time. We see Christ present in our brothers and sisters, in the young and old, men and women, rich and poor, people of all nations. We see Christ and are gathered by him into the one Body through the ministry of the priest who presides as Christ at our assembly.

The Liturgy of the Word enables us to hear the Lord speak to our hearts and minds through Sacred Scripture proclaimed by his ministers. His words come to our own lips as we join in the proclamation of the Responsorial Psalm. The priest assists in our finding nourishment in the Word, through the breaking of the bread of the Word in the homily.

In the Eucharistic Prayer for Various Needs and Occasions we acknowledge these various presences, giving thanks to God the Father and thanks for God the Son.

You are indeed Holy and to be glorified, O God,
who love the human race

and who always walk with us on the journey of life.
Blessed indeed is your Son,
present in our midst
when we are gathered by his love
and when, as once for the disciples, so now for us,
he opens the Scriptures and breaks the bread.

The celebration of the Liturgy of the Word prepares us for the central action of the Mass, **the Liturgy of the Eucharist**, for the prayer of Thanksgiving in which the Sacrifice of Jesus becomes present in the act of consecration, through the ministry of the priest, is re-presented to the Father, and then shared with us in Holy Communion.

Thus nourished, thus sustained, in the **Concluding Rites** the community prays, grateful for what has been shared with it and knowing itself newly called to be the Body of Christ for the World.

Christ present in the Eucharistic species

Catholic theology and devotion finds a particular focus in the presence of Christ in the Eucharistic species, the sacramental food and drink that are his Body and Blood

The mode of Christ's presence under the Eucharistic species is unique. It raises the Eucharist above all the sacraments as 'the perfection of the spiritual life and the end to which all the sacraments tend.' In the most blessed sacrament of the Eucharist 'the body and blood, together with the soul and divinity, of our Lord Jesus Christ and, therefore, the whole Christ is truly, really, and substantially contained.' 'This presence is called "real" - by which is not intended to exclude the other types of presence as if they could not be "real" too, but because it is presence in the fullest sense: that is to say, it is a substantial presence by which Christ, God and man, makes himself wholly and entirely present.'

It is by the conversion of the bread and wine into Christ's Body and Blood that Christ becomes present in this sacrament. The Church Fathers strongly affirmed the faith of the Church in the efficacy of the word of Christ and of the action of the Holy Spirit to bring about this conversion. Thus St John Chrysostom declares:

> It is not man that causes the things offered to become the Body and Blood of Christ, but he who was crucified for us, Christ himself. The priest, in the role of Christ, pronounces these words, but their power and grace are God's. This is my body, he says. This word transforms the things offered.

The Council of Trent summarizes the Catholic faith by declaring: 'Because Christ our Redeemer said that it was truly his body that he was offering under the species of bread, it has always been the conviction of the Church of God, and this holy Council now declares again, that by the consecration of the bread and wine there takes place a change of the whole substance of the bread into the substance of the body of Christ our Lord and of the whole substance of the wine into the substance of his blood. This change the holy Catholic Church has fittingly and properly called transubstantiation.'

CCC 1374, 1375, 1376

Worship of the Eucharist outside of Mass

The substantial character of Christ's presence in the Eucharistic species, and the practice of reserving the sacramental food in order to be able to take Holy Communion to the sick and dying, makes it possible for the faithful to gather in Christ's Eucharistic presence for private prayer (or indeed prayer in common) outside from Mass.

A particular feature of the devotional life of the Catholic Church, this form of prayer allows for communion:

The devotion prompting the faithful to visit the blessed sacrament draws them into an ever deeper share in the Paschal Mystery and leads them to respond gratefully to the gift of him who through his humanity constantly pours divine life into the members of his Body. Abiding with Christ the Lord, they enjoy his intimate friendship and pour out their hearts before him for themselves and for those dear to them and they pray for the peace and salvation of the world. Offering their entire lives with Christ to the Father in the Holy Spirit, they derive from this sublime colloquy an increase of faith, hope, and charity. Thus they foster those right dispositions that enable them with due devotion to celebrate the memorial of the Lord and receive frequently the bread given us by the Father.

Prayer before Christ the Lord sacramentally present extends the union with Christ that the faithful have reached in communion. It renews the covenant that in turn moves them to maintain by the way they live what they have received through faith and the sacrament. They should strive to lead their whole lives in the strength of this heavenly food, as sharers in the death and resurrection of the Lord. All should be eager to do good works and to please God, so that they may seek to imbue the world with the Christian spirit and, in all things, even in the midst of human affairs, to become witnesses of Christ.

General Introduction to the *Rites for Holy Communion and worship of the Eucharist outside Mass*, 80, 81

Praying with the Scriptures outside of Mass

Prayer and worship with the Scriptures outside of Mass was encouraged at the Second Vatican Council (SC 35.5). This prayer can take many different forms - the Bible services envisaged by *Sacrosanctum Concilium*, celebrations of a Liturgy of the Word; *Lectio divina*; celebrations of the Divine Office. It helps to deepen people's knowledge and love of the Scriptures, and further to assist their participation in the Mass.

Taking things further

Bring each mode of Christ's personal presence to mind and heart, and reflect on them in prayer.

- How do the Introductory Rites help you to be ready for the 'meat' of the Mass?

- What helps and hinders your being nourished by the Liturgy of the Word?

- Which parts of the Liturgy of the Eucharist particular engage you? Are there parts that you find less notable or even neglect?

- How do the Concluding Rites help us understand the mission of the Church, a mission in which we share?

- When are there opportunities in your daily or weekly routine for times of prayer nourished by the word of God and/or prayer before the Blessed Sacrament?

The Liturgy of the Mass as it relates to the Ministry of Holy Communion

Having taken a broader over view of the Mass, we now look at aspects of the Mass that particularly relate to the ministry of Holy Communion.

We will look in greater detail at the Liturgy of the Eucharist and, in particular, the rite of Holy Communion as this is where the ministry is principally carried out. But we will also look at other things which relate to the ministry of Holy Communion, as sometimes the minister will be asked to assist the community more broadly than at Mass only.

Perhaps the first thing to note is the significance, from the New Testament onwards, of the two usages of the phrase 'The Body of Christ'.

The Body of Christ:
Sacrament of Jesus, Sacrament of the Church

St Paul is the first to write of how Jesus spoke of the bread of the Last Supper, over which he gave thanks, which he broke and gave to the disciples, as having become his body (1 *Co* 11:23-26).

St Paul also speaks of the Church, the Christian community, as having become the body of Christ (1 *Co*

12.12-27; *Rm* 12:4-5); of Christ being the head, but us together with him being the body (*Ep* 1:22-23; 4:11-16).

These are two modes of bodily presence and both clearly different but, also, both really Christ: Christ present in the Eucharistic food (and drink) that is his Body and Blood, and Christ present in the Church, that is his Body.

St Augustine

The great teacher of this mystery, after St Paul himself, is St Augustine. Bishop of Hippo in North Africa in the mid-fifth century, Augustine offered these words of instruction to the newly baptised, reflecting with them on the deeper meaning of their communion with Christ through baptism, in the Church, and their communion with him in the Eucharist, which they are to receive for the first time.

If you want to understand the body of Christ,
listen to the Apostle Paul speaking to the faithful:
'You are the body of Christ, member for member.'
[1 *Co* 12.27]
If you, therefore, are Christ's body and members,
it is your own mystery that is placed on the
Lord's table!
It is your own mystery that you are receiving!
You are saying 'Amen' to what you are
your response is a personal signature,
affirming your faith.

When you hear 'The body of Christ' you reply 'Amen.'
Be a member of Christ's body, then,
so that your 'Amen' may ring true!
But what role does the bread play?

We have no theory of our own to propose here;
listen, instead, to what Paul says about this sacrament:
'The bread is one, and we, though many, are one body.'
[1 Co 10.17]
Understand and rejoice: unity, truth, faithfulness, love.
'One bread,' he says. What is this one bread?
Is it not the 'one body,' formed from many?
Remember: bread doesn't come from a single grain,
but from many.
When you received exorcism, you were 'ground.'
When you were baptized, you were 'leavened.'
When you received the fire of the Holy Spirit,
you were 'baked.'
Be what you see; receive what you are.
This is what Paul is saying about the bread.
So too, what we are to understand about the cup
is similar and requires little explanation.
In the visible object of bread,
many grains are gathered into one
just as the faithful (so Scripture says)
form 'a single heart and mind in God' [Ac 4.32]

And thus it is with the wine.
Remember, friends, how wine is made

individual grapes hang together in a bunch,
but the juice from them all is mingled to become
a single brew.
This is the image chosen by Christ our Lord
to show how, at his own table,
the mystery of our unity and peace
is solemnly consecrated.
All who fail to keep the bond of peace
after entering this mystery
receive not a sacrament that benefits them,
but an indictment that condemns them.

So let us give God our sincere and deepest gratitude
and, as far as human weakness will permit,
let us turn to the Lord with pure hearts.
With all our strength, let us seek God's singular mercy,
for then the Divine Goodness will surely
hear our prayers.
God's power will drive the Evil One from our acts
and thoughts;
it will deepen our faith, govern our minds,
grant us holy thoughts,
and lead us, finally, to share the divine happiness
through God's own son Jesus Christ. Amen!

'A Homily by St Augustine, Bishop of Hippo'
Latin text in J.-P. Migne, *Patrologia Latina* 38
1246-1248; translated by Nathan D. Mitchell.
Assembly Vol 23:2, March 1997.

Ministering Communion at Mass

The privilege of the minister is to serve these two communions: ministering the Holy Communion that is the sacrament of Christ's Body and Blood to the Holy Communion of the Church.

The dynamic setting where this most usually takes place is during the celebration of the Mass.

We are all familiar with the priest's words in Eucharistic Prayer III:

Look, we pray, upon the oblation of your Church
and recognizing the sacrificial Victim by whose death
you willed to reconcile us to yourself,
grant that we, who are nourished
by the Body and Blood of your Son
and filled with his Holy Spirit,
may become one body, one spirit in Christ

(*Roman Missal*, The Order of Mass, 113)

More expressive yet are the words of the Eucharistic Prayer for use in Masses for Various Needs:

Therefore, holy Father,
as we celebrate the memorial of Christ your Son,
    our Saviour,
whom you led through his Passion and Death
    on the Cross
to the glory of the Resurrection,
and whom you have seated at your right hand,

we proclaim the work of your love until he comes again
and we offer you the Bread of life
and the Chalice of blessing.

Look with favour on the oblation of your Church,
in which we show forth
the paschal Sacrifice of Christ that has been handed
    on to us,
and grant that, by the power of the Spirit of your love,
we may be counted now and until the day of eternity
among the members of your Son,
in whose Body and Blood we have communion.
Bring your Church, O Lord,
to perfect faith and charity,
together with N. our Pope and N. our Bishop,
with all Bishops, Priests and Deacons,
and the entire people you have made your own.

Open our eyes to the needs of our brothers and sisters;
inspire in us words and actions
to comfort those who labour and are burdened.
Make us serve them truly,
after the example of Christ and at his command.
And may your Church stand as a living witness
to truth and freedom, to peace and justice,
that all people may be raised up to a new hope.

Roman Missal, Appendix to the Order of Mass:Eucharistic
          Prayer for use in Masses for Various Needs III 7.

We have communion in the Body of Christ. It is ours as we share in the communion between God the Father and God the Son, expressed in his Sacrifice and shared with us in the sacrament of the Bread of life and the Chalice of Blessing. United in Christ, we are called to serve the Body of Christ, and our every neighbour.

Encouraged by this rich metaphorical and sacramental language let us look at the Liturgy of the Mass and see how it relates to the ministry of Communion.

The Principal Parts of the Mass

Introductory Rites

The principal function of the Introductory Rites is:

> to ensure that the faithful, who come together as one, establish communion and dispose themselves properly to listen to the word of God and to celebrate the Eucharist worthily.

GIRM 46

These rites serve as spiritual exercises in repentance, thanksgiving and praise. They are like the warm-up exercises of an athlete for those coming to do the work of the Liturgy and to be joined with the prayer of the Church. Serving the whole assembly in this way, they are of particular importance to the one to whom is asked to minister the word prayerfully, faithfully and fruitfully.

The minister of Holy Communion should take an interest in the way the community gathers. If we gather as strangers, unwelcomed, maybe we will remain that way, despite the Mass. Ministers of Holy Communion will not necessarily themselves serve also as ministers of welcome and hospitality. However they will want to try and ensure that these other ministries are exercised for the sake of the fruitfulness of the Mass in the life of their community.

Liturgy of the Word

The word is spoken to bring to mind and engage us afresh in the history of salvation. The Eucharist which is the sacramental fulfilment of the word offers the sacrifice of praise to God and makes available to us the fulness of redemption.

The more we are nourished by the word, the more we will hunger for its fulfilment by grace, even in our lives, and so the better prepared we will be to receive the sacrament of the Eucharist, and the more ready to share it fittingly with others through our ministry.

In the Prayer of the Faithful, the Body of Christ unites in silent prayer for the intentions proposed by the reader. In the stillness of those pauses for prayer, when each member of the congregation prays in their own way for the intention of all, the diversity of the Church expresses itself in a powerful and often moving way in unity of purpose and care.

Liturgy of the Eucharist

Sometimes our sense for the meaning of Holy Communion can be narrowed to a single focus on our own relationship with the Lord. Being attentive to the content of the Eucharistic Prayers will help us remain open to the breadth of Eucharistic prayer.

The following table uses Eucharistic Prayer II to demonstrate that breadth. You might like to similarly examine the Missal's other Eucharistic Prayers, of which there are effectively nine - Eucharistic Prayers I, III and IV, the two Eucharistic prayers for Reconciliation and the four forms of the Eucharistic Prayer for Various Needs - for private prayer and reflection. Note the great richness of expression of thanksgiving, praise and intercession.

EUCHARISTIC PRAYER II	
V. The Lord be with you. R. **And with your spirit.** V. Lift up your hearts. R. **We lift them up to the Lord.** V. Let us give thanks to the Lord our God. R. **It is right and just.**	Led by the priest, the gathered community is united in a common action. The priest does not pray alone, and the assembly is not without its priest who presides as *alter Christus*.

It is truly right and just, our duty and our salvation, always and everywhere to give you thanks, Father most holy, through your beloved Son, Jesus Christ, your Word through whom you made all things, whom you sent as our Saviour and Redeemer, incarnate by the Holy Spirit and born of the Virgin.

Fulfilling your will and gaining for you a holy people, he stretched out his hands as he endured his Passion, so as to break the bonds of death and manifest the resurrection.

And so, with the Angels and all the Saints we declare your glory, as with one voice we acclaim:

Holy, Holy, Holy Lord God of hosts. Heaven and earth are full of your glory. Hosanna in the highest. Blessed is he who comes in the name of the Lord. Hosanna in the highest.

The Preface states the particular reason for the prayer offered - often a particular feast or season, or a particular occasion - a wedding, a funeral, or simply, as here, because of our thankfulness for Jesus Christ.

Its conclusion and the Sanctus which follows reminds that this particular assembly prays united with saints and angels in its participation in the Sacrifice of Christ.

100. *The Priest, with hands extended, says*: You are indeed Holy, O Lord, the fount of all holiness.	The words of the priest continue to be addressed to God the Father – to whom Jesus offered himself for the salvation of the world.
101. *He joins his hands and, holding them extended over the offerings, says*: Make holy, therefore, these gifts, we pray, by sending down your Spirit upon them like the dewfall, *He joins his hands and makes the Sign of the Cross once over the bread and the chalice together, saying*: so that they may become for us the Body and ✠ Blood of our Lord Jesus Christ.	The Holy Spirit is invoked and called down upon the gifts of bread and wine for their transformation. The Spirit who participated in the first Creation has a key role in bringing to birth of a new creation in Christ.
102. At the time he was betrayed and entered willingly into his Passion, *He takes the bread and, holding it slightly raised above the altar, continues*: he took bread and, giving thanks, broke it, and gave it to his disciples, saying: *He bows slightly.* TAKE THIS, ALL OF YOU, AND EAT OF IT, FOR THIS IS MY BODY, WHICH WILL BE GIVEN UP FOR YOU.	The words of the Institution Narrative, reminding of the words, action and meaning of the Last Supper are consecratory. Through them, by the working of the Holy Spirit through the ministry of the priest, the 'past' event of the Paschal Mystery – the Passion, Death and Rising of Jesus – becomes present reality.

He shows the consecrated host to the people, places it again on the paten, and genuflects in adoration.

103. *After this, he continues:*
In a similar way, when supper was ended,
He takes the chalice and, holding it slightly raised above the altar, continues:
he took the chalice
and, once more giving thanks,
he gave it to his disciples, saying:

He bows slightly.

TAKE THIS, ALL OF YOU,
AND DRINK FROM IT,
FOR THIS IS THE CHALICE
OF MY BLOOD,
THE BLOOD OF THE NEW
AND ETERNAL COVENANT,
WHICH WILL BE POURED
OUT FOR YOU AND
FOR MANY
FOR THE FORGIVENESS
OF SINS.
DO THIS IN MEMORY OF ME.

He shows the chalice to the people , places it in the corporal, and genuflects in adoration.

The highpoint of the Eucharistic Prayer (EP) is still to come but already Christ is present, and the community is offered the opportunity to gaze on his sacramental presence in what was only bread and wine, but is now his Body and Blood.

104. *Then he says*:
The mystery of faith.
And the people continue,
acclaiming:
We proclaim your Death,
O Lord,
and profess your Resurrection
until you come again.
          Or:
When we eat this Bread
and drink this Cup,
we proclaim your Death,
O Lord, until you come again.
          Or:
Save us, Saviour of the world,
for by your Cross and
Resurrection you have set
us free.

The words sung professing the Mystery of Faith express not only the Paschal Mystery, but our trust and hope that this is a saving mystery for us and for others.

105. *Then the Priest, with hands extended, says*:
Therefore, as we celebrate the memorial of his Death and Resurrection, we offer you, Lord, the Bread of life and the Chalice of salvation, giving thanks that you have held us worthy to be in your presence and minister to you. Humbly we pray that, partaking of the Body and Blood of Christ, we may be gathered into one by the Holy Spirit.

The simple sung phrases in which we profess our faith in the saving mystery of Christ's Dying and Rising are amplified in the formal memorial (*anamnesis*) of the Prayer.

In particular we pray for a deepening of our communion with Christ in the Church, by the Holy Spirit.

Remember, Lord, your Church,
spread throughout the world,
and bring her to the fulness of
charity,
together with N. our Pope and
N. our Bishop
and all the clergy.

*In Masses for the Dead, the
following may be added*:
Remember your servant N.,
whom you have called (today)
from this world to yourself.
Grant that he (she) who was
united with your Son in a death
like his,
may also be one with him in his
Resurrection.

Remember also our brothers and
sisters who have fallen asleep in
the hope of the resurrection,
and all who have died in your
mercy: welcome them into the
light of your face.
Have mercy on us all, we pray,
that with the Blessed Virgin
Mary, Mother of God, with the
blessed Apostles,
and all the Saints who have
pleased you throughout the ages,
we may merit to be coheirs to
eternal life, and may praise and
glorify you
through your Son, Jesus Christ.

When we pray the Eucharistic
Prayer we do not pray alone:
already we have seen how we
pray united with Christ, and with
angels and saints.
Neither do we pray for ourselves
alone – but for the whole Church
and for the world also.

This prayer finds its fullest
expression in the fourth form of
the Eucharistic Prayer for use in
Masses for Various Needs,
as noted above (pp.29-30.)

106. *He takes the chalice and the paten with the host and, raising both, he says:* Through him, and with him, and in him, O God, almighty Father, in the unity of the Holy Spirit, all glory and honour is yours, for ever and ever. *The people acclaim:* **Amen.**	The culmination of the Eucharistic Prayer is the concluding Doxology where the Church's offering of itself and its praise is visible united in the re-presentation to the Father of the Sacrifice of Christ.

The Eucharistic Prayer is in many respects the high point of the Mass – it is the re-presentation of the Sacrifice, it is the occasion for Christ's substantial presence among us; it is the most formal expression of the prayer of the Church. In more recent years, as the reception of Holy Communion has become more common, the importance of the Prayer has maybe been somewhat obscured, displaced by the action of receiving Communion. However, without properly appreciating what the Eucharistic Prayer is all about, the meaning of Holy Communion itself is put in jeopardy.

Communion Rite

The first actions of the Communion Rite help members of the assembly prepare to receive Holy Communion. The minister of Holy Communion, of course, prepares not only to receive communion themselves, but also for the privilege of assisting in the distribution of Holy Communion to other members of the Assembly and, sometimes, of taking Holy Communion from Mass to those who are sick or infirm and unable to attend the Mass themselves. This can bring an additional dimension to the prayerful preparation.

Not all members of the assembly will receive Holy Communion. Often a minister will be asked to minister a blessing to someone who has not yet been admitted to Communion, or who is of another faith, or not receiving for some other reason. Guidance regarding these blessings is given in the next chapter.

The practice of Spiritual Communion has been rather neglected over past years. However it is something that has received new attention recently as something helpful for those unable to be invited to receive Holy Communion in the usual way. Again, it is discussed further in the next chapter. Ministers should be ready to discuss the practice of Spiritual Communion with members of the Church as the occasion presents itself. They would do well also at Mass to remember in prayer those who do not receive Communion, praying for the time when all will be perfectly united in Christ.

Concluding Rites

The Mass is celebrated so that we may more fully become the Body of Christ for the world. As a minister of Communion, it is good to make a point of praying for the members of the community at this point of the Mass, praying that they will be faithful to their mission, the mission of the Church.

Other aspects of liturgy and catechesis related to the ministry of Holy Communion

Holy Communion and Worship of the Eucharist outside of Mass

Worship of the Eucharist outside of Mass has a privileged place in Catholic worship and devotion. It is a practice that ministers of Holy Communion do well to cultivate to better support their own relationship with Christ in the Eucharist. Ministers may find themselves called on to minister to their brothers and sisters through these forms of worship also.

Communion to the Sick

The work of the minister of Communion in building up and sustaining the communion of the Church is clearest in their ministry to those who cannot gather for Mass with the rest of the community. Responding to their need the minister takes word and sacrament to them. The simple rite for the Communion of the Sick is given in pages 56-60 below, and appears in its full detail in the ritual book *The Pastoral Care of the Sick*.

Guidance as to the safeguarding of those visited, and the minister, will be provided by each parish and diocese. Often it is suggested that two ministers should attend, a minister of the word, and a minister of Holy Communion. This can be very helpful, and help ensure that if, on occasion, one minister is not able to attend the ministry can be continued by the other, for the benefit of the sick person.

It is helpful if the ministry team meets together with the parish priest, perhaps quarterly, to ensure that broader pastoral needs are considered, and that there is proper accountability for the ministry carried out in the name of the Church.

Exposition of the Blessed Sacrament

Prayer before Christ sacramentally present in the Blessed Sacrament can take place in a number of forms. Perhaps the most common is simply prayer before the Blessed Sacrament reserved in the tabernacle. However especially prized is prayer before the Blessed Sacrament exposed in a monstrance as part of a Holy Hour or more extended time of exposition.

Commonly this latter form of worship concludes with Benediction, with a priest or deacon making the sign of the cross over the congregation with the Blessed Sacrament contained in the monstrance.

However in the absence of a priest or deacon a commissioned minister of Holy Communion may expose and later repose the Holy Eucharist for the adoration of the faithful.

Celebrations of the Word and Holy Communion

This form of celebration is principally intended for communities who cannot celebrate Mass on Sundays.[6] In the absence of a priest the Bishop can authorise a lay minister to lead the community in its worship of God, and also authorise the distribution of Holy Communion. Often it will be a deacon or a minister of the word who will be the best person to preside at the Liturgy, however, in the absence of a deacon, or when the deacon needs assistance, parish commissioned ministers of communion may also assist.

Catechesis

Ministers of Holy Communion with a deep love for the Eucharist, active in liturgical and pastoral ministry, can often be a helpful resource for the parish's catechetical work – either in preparing young people for their first Communion, teenagers for Confirmation, or adults for Baptism and Eucharist (entry into full communion with the Church). They will also have a particular perspective to bring to the Church's work of the new evangelisation[7], helping those already members of the Church to know and live their faith more fully, and helping to spread the good news still further beyond the obvious bounds of their community.

Guidelines for Ministers of Holy Communion at Mass, and related liturgies

Training

It is important that ministers of Holy Communion have a good understanding of the ministry that they share in, and especially of the Mystery of the Holy Eucharist.

In selecting people to exercise ministry as commissioned ministers of Holy Communion, the parish priest will generally look for someone whose faith is evident, who is of good character and respected in the community. This helps to ensure that there is no contradiction between who and how the minister is in themselves and the Mystery of Communion that they are called to minister.

Most of those called to serve as commissioned ministers, like most of those called to serve as bishops, priests and deacons, know that they are not worthy of the call. And yet others recognise in us something that we may not recognise for ourselves. If asked to serve then unless there is some grave reason not to do so, we can confidently accept the invitation, trusting in the Church, and in the love of God. We will require some instruction in the ministry, but the most important qualities are likely to be already in place.

What particular instruction are we likely to need? The basics are simply these - the practical details about how to minister Holy Communion (under both kinds, and how to minister the host in the hand and on the tongue) and in the particular parish that one is commissioned to serve - for example when to come to the sanctuary, where to stand to receive Communion, where to stand when distributing Holy Communion, what to do with the Communion vessels (and any remaining hosts or Precious Blood) when the congregation has received Communion; and to be clear what to do should there be some accident: if, for instance, a chalice or hosts are dropped – such things very rarely happen, but knowing what to do can make any accident less upsetting for everyone concerned, should it come to it.

There are, of course, also many other things that it is useful for a minister of Holy Communion to know and be introduced to, including the following. Some of them are likely to be part of an induction course for new ministers, and all are likely to be explored as part of the ongoing formation programme provided for ministers in the parish, deanery and diocese.

The Eucharist

- The themes of Covenant and Sacrifice in the Scriptures
- The history of the Mass and worship of the Eucharist outside of Mass

- The theology of Sacrament

The Church

- The nature and mission of the Church
- The ministries of the Church

The Liturgy

- The relationship between word and Sacrament
- Liturgical ministry
- Relationship between worship and mission

Being a minister

- At Mass
- At services of Exposition
- As a minister to people who are sick or housebound
- Collaboration

Additional training will be needed for those who are regularly ministering people who are sick (dealing with spiritual accompaniment, and safeguarding issues) and those who are leading worship (e.g. more detailed consideration of particular forms of liturgy and the Liturgical Year, as well as presiding skills).

Practical Guidance for ministers at Mass

Preparation beforehand

An obvious thing, but worth saying: it is important to have clean hands for ministering Holy Communion. If necessary, wash your hands in the sacristy before Mass begins.

Arriving in time

Ministers work as members of a team, and it is an act of courtesy to the team, as well as to the wider congregation to make sure they arrive in good time for the celebration of the Liturgy.

It is good practice to have a method of 'signing-in', and also an agreed time by which all ministers will have either signed in or been replaced by another minister.

Prayerful preparation

In the final minutes before Mass, pray privately for a moment or two for the community you are there to serve. Pray that their reception of Holy Communion may be fruitful for their lives.

The ministry team may also assemble in the sacristy to pray with the priest before Mass begins, and to form part of the entrance procession.

It may be helpful to note the order of ministers in the entrance procession:

- the thurifer carrying a smoking thurible, if incense is being used

- servers who carry lighted candles, and between them a server carrying the processional cross

- others ministers (eg servers, readers, cantors and commissioned ministers of Holy Communion)

- a reader carrying a Book of the Gospels, slightly elevated;

- the Priest who is to celebrate the Mass.

Those ministers who are not to be seated on the sanctuary will genuflect at entrance to the sanctuary (if the Blessed Sacrament is reserved there) and then make their way to their place. If the Blessed Sacrament is not reserved on the sanctuary, they will simply bow to the altar before making their way to their place.

Entering and leaving the sanctuary during Mass

Locally agreed practice will observed as to what ministers of Holy Commnion should wear when ministering (the basic choices are modest street clothing or an alb, but always clean and smart); whether all ministers come to and leave the sanctuary at the same time, or not; where to stand to receive Holy Communion; and where to stand to distribute Holy Communion.

Even if the Blessed Sacrament is reserved in the sanctuary ministers should not genuflect on entering/leaving the sanctuary: rather the minister should bow to the altar.

Distributing Holy Communion

Distributing the Host

The two normal ways of receiving the host in England and Wales, commended by the Bishops, are either in the hand or directly on the tongue. The choice as to which of these ways to receive is left to the communicant – both are always acceptable.In both cases, before ministering the host, the minister says: 'The Body of Christ' and the communicant responds 'Amen.'

- *In the hand* - When receiving Holy Communion in the hand, we make with our hands the form of both a cross and a throne in which to receive our King who sacrificed his life for us. With clean, empty hands and with gloves removed, we receive him with utter reverence and consume the Host carefully in the presence of the minister before turning away.[8]

- *On the tongue* - When we receive Holy Communion on the tongue, we are aware of coming to be fed with the Food of Life, conscious of our utter dependence on the Lord. We know the holiness of the One we receive, beyond our touch.[9]

Distributing the Precious Blood

By tradition a deacon is a minister of the chalice, and will exercise that ministry even where there is a mix of ordained and lay ministers assisting with the distribution of Holy Communion.

Before ministering the chalice, the minister says: 'The Blood of Christ' and the communicant responds 'Amen.'

The minister should hand the chalice to the communicant who should receive it with two hands and return it to the minister.

The minister then wipes the outside of the chalice with the purificator cloth, and turns the chalice by a quarter turn before presenting it to the next communicant.

Intinction

Receiving Holy Communion by Intinction, where the host is dipped into the Precious Blood by the minister and placed directly by them on the tongue of the communicant, is discouraged in England and Wales. It obscures the distinct fulfilment of the invitation of the Lord to take and eat, to take and drink.

The Bishops have said that 'If Communion under both kinds is given by intinction (which is not recommended in England and Wales), the communicant may choose to receive under the form of bread only. When Communion in the form of intinction is given, the following formula is said, "The Body and Blood of Christ," and the communicant responds, "Amen". Intinction can only be administered by a minister and may not be self-administered.'[10]

Blessing those who do not receive Holy Communion

Often people will present themselves for a blessing during the Communion Procession. They will sometimes be Christians who are not Catholic or Orthodox, or Catholics who for some reason are not asking for Communion. Sometimes they will be people of other faiths (or none) who have come to join the Church in prayer for some reason or another.

Over recent years it has been common for such people to be invited to receive a blessing during the Communion Rite.

The Church has not laid down any guidelines for the form of the blessing. However two principles are widely observed.

First, that the form of blessing during the Communion Rite should be the same whether given by an ordained minister or a lay minister. This should discourage all those wanting a blessing going to one class of minister or the other.

For that reason, and secondly, the blessing takes the form of a prayer, rather than the typical form of blessing such as that which concludes the Mass, ie 'May almighty God bless you, the Father, the Son, and the Holy Spirit'. That form of blessing is reserved to the clergy.

So, a better form for use during the Communion Rite would be the prayer:

> May the love of God be in your heart always.

Or the biblical phrase:

> May the Lord let his face shine on you
> and be gracious to you.[11]

The minister may place their hand on the head or the shoulder of the person being prayed for, before saying the prayer.

After the distribution of Holy Communion

A minister of the chalice should return the chalice to the altar or credence table as parish practice determines. Any remaining consecrated wine should be consumed by the priest, and the lay ministers return to their places.

If any hosts are remaining they will be gathered together and then (if there are a very few) be consumed by the priest or placed in the tabernacle by one of the ministers of communion, clergy or lay.

The purification of the communion vessels, cleansing them with water and drying them, should be carried out by an ordained minister. If there are many vessels then this purification may be better carried out after the end of Mass.

Dismissal of Commissioned Ministers taking Communion
to the Housebound or Sick

It is fitting for Holy Communion to be taken directly from Mass to the sick or those unable to leave their homes.

The pyx may be prepared at the end of the distribution of Holy Communion and left on the corporal ready to be formally given to the ministers concerned.

Appropriate times for the deacons, acolytes, or commissioned ministers of Holy Communion to receive a pyx from the priest and be 'sent' to take Holy Communion and leave the assembly are either after the Communion of the people or immediately before the final blessing.

The ministers may depart before the Prayer after Communion, immediately after the Prayer after Communion or as part of the concluding procession of ministers. Local circumstances will determine which of these various options will be most fitting in any particular parish.

The Presider will normally speak words of dismissal or missioning over the ministers taking Holy Communion to the sick and housebound. These words may be based on the words of the Communion antiphon, on the readings of the day, or in a simple form such as:

Go now, to our sisters and brothers unable to be with us for reasons of sickness and infirmity. Take to them from our celebration the word of God and Holy Communion, that they might share with us these signs of the Lord's goodness.[12]

Additional notes

Being personally present

The minister is ministering to the faithful, not merely distributing Holy Communion, so the action of ministering needs to be, to some extent, a person-to-person engagement. Of course the principal focus of the engagement is the mutual relationship with Christ present in the Sacrament, but attentiveness to the person to whom you are ministering is most appropriate also. This might be expressed most commonly by making eye contact as you say 'The Body of Christ', in listening to their response, in waiting for them to be ready to receive; acknowledging the presence of a child, and so on. A warm personal human presence provides an appropriate context for someone to receive the living and loving Lord in Holy Communion.

Taking appropriate responsibility for any irregularity

It is very rare for someone to come to receive communion who should not, or who wishes to abuse the Sacrament, but it does happen. If someone receives the host and goes to walk away with it simply ask them, gently but firmly, to consume it directly. In most cases they will have simply been distracted and will comply immediately. Sometimes however it will become evident that the person is not familiar with receiving communion. In that case it is better to take the host from them (and consume it yourself or put it to one side as described below, cf 'Accidents with Hosts') and offer a blessing. Try to speak to the person after the Mass also just to explain, so that they are helped to know what to do next time they are at Mass, and to resolve any embarrassment caused.

If the matter is not resolved easily draw it to the attention of the priest presiding at the Mass, during the Communion Rite or afterwards, as seems best.

Accidents

Again it is very rare, but it happens, that a host or hosts or a chalice are dropped.

Accidents with the consecrated wine

If the chalice is dropped then a purificator or purificators should be placed over any spilt consecrated wine to soak it up. Normally this should be left in place until after the Mass has ended when the floor can be properly cleaned and the purificators dealt in the appropriate way.

If the consecrated wine has spilt on someone's clothing, then they should be provided with a purificator to dab it from their clothes, and where appropriate they should be given access to the sacristy so that water can be used to remove the consecrated wine. It is better that this should be done directly over the *sacrarium* so that the water used may drain directly to the earth, thus best respecting the dignity of the sacramental species.

Accidents with Hosts

If a host is dropped on a clean floor, then usually the simplest way to deal with the 'problem' is for the minister to pick up the host and consume it directly.

If that is not suitable then the host should be put to one side (perhaps held in the minister's hand, or returned directly to the altar and left on the corporal) until the minister has finished distributing Holy Communion. The priest should be then told what has happened. Commonly he will then remove the host to the sacristy and dissolve it in water, pouring the water into the *sacrarium*, returning it directly to the earth.

The same procedure should be followed whether the accident involved a single host or a number of hosts.

Ministering Holy Communion to the sick
in Hospital or in their home

The rite to be used in ministering Holy Communion to the Sick is contained in the ritual book *Pastoral Care of the Sick*. Those ministers who are regularly ministering to the sick should have their own copy of the rite.[13]

The outline of the Rite of ministering Holy Communion to the Sick is as follows:

Introductory Rites

Greeting

The minister greets the sick person and others present. An ordained minister will use the standard form as used at Mass. A lay minister will instead say:

Brothers and sisters, let us bless the Lord,
who went about doing good
and healing the sick.

Blessed be God now and for ever.
R. Blessed be God now and for ever. *Or:* **Amen.**

Penitential Act

One of the forms provided in the Missal is used. The third form is perhaps the simplest only requiring the sick person to respond to the Lord, have mercy/Christ, have mercy, eg

Lord Jesus, you healed the sick:
Lord, have mercy. **Lord, have mercy.**

Lord Jesus, you forgave sinners:
Christ, have mercy. **Christ, have mercy.**

Lord Jesus, you give us yourself
to heal us and bring us strength:
Lord, have mercy. **Lord, have mercy.**

The minister concludes the Penitential Act with the usual absolution.

Liturgy of the Word

Reading

The word of God is proclaimed by one of those present or by the minister. The Gospel of the Day or the Sunday may be used, or alternatively a Gospel passage from the selection provided in Appendix

Response

The response to the word of God may take the form of a brief silence or words of reflection by the minister.

General Intercessions

The text used at Mass that Sunday may be used, or a simplified form suited to the circumstances of the person being ministered to

Liturgy of Holy Communion

The Lord's Prayer

Communion

The minister shows the Host to those present using approved words, such as those used at Mass:

> Behold the Lamb of God,
> behold him who takes away the sins of the world.
> Blessed are those called
> to the supper of the Lamb.

**Lord, I am not worthy
that you should enter under my roof,
but only say the word
and my soul shall be healed.**

*Holy Communion is then ministered in the usual way to the
sick person, and others present who wish to receive.*

Silent Prayer

Prayer after Communion

*The minister says a concluding prayer. The prayer used at
Mass that day or on the preceding Sunday may be suitable,
but may also need adjusting for use outside of Mass.
Alternatively the following prayer might be used.*

God our Father,
you have called us to share
the one bread and one cup
and so become one in Christ.

Help us to live in him,
that we may bear fruit,
rejoicing that he has redeemed the world.

We ask this through Christ our Lord.

Amen.

Concluding Rite

Blessing

An ordained minister will offer a blessing in the usual way. A lay minister will invoke God's blessing and make the sign of the cross on himself or herself while saying a prayer for blessing such as:

> May the Lord bless us,
> protect us from all evil
> and bring us to everlasting life.
> **Amen.**

The minister is likely to find themselves having to minister in all sorts of different circumstances, and will need to be adaptable. However it is good to try to ensure that the setting for ministering Holy Communion is always worthy and reverent.

If Holy Communion is being taken to someone who is housebound but within their home relatively independent, they might be gently encouraged, as they prepare for the visit of the minister, to prepare a table where the pyx can be placed during the first part of the service. It would be helpful if they can prepare a table covered with a clean white cloth on the table, with a crucifix, and have a candle ready to light.

Failing that, the minister can make sure they take with them a small cross, a clean purificator, and even a candle.

Sometimes, of course, even this may not be possible - for example if visiting someone in hospital.

However, always try to establish an environment suitable for prayer. If a television is on, ask whether it might be switched off for the time of prayer. Use a brief time of silence to gather your thoughts and theirs before beginning.

Sometimes it is most appropriate to minister Holy Communion at the very beginning of a visit. At other times it will be better to take some time in conversation. Often such conversation will suggest intentions for intercessions during the time of prayer.

Ministers will always want to do what is best for the person they are ministering to. Sometimes that is achieved by using the full rite, sometimes by abbreviating it. Such an abbreviation is anticipated in the *Pastoral Care of the Sick*, where a form of the rite without a Liturgy of the Word is provided for the ministering of Holy Communion in a Hospital or Institution.

The briefer rite is as follows:

Introductory Rite

Antiphon[14]

Liturgy of Holy Communion

Greeting
The Lord's Prayer
Communion

Concluding Rite

Concluding Prayer

ASSISTING AT A SERVICE OF EXPOSITION
OF THE BLESSED SACRAMENT

The rite to be used is contained in the ritual book *Holy Communion and Worship of the Eucharist outside Mass*.

When it is led by a commissioned minister, the outline of the rite is as follows. The ritual book offers clear guidance on the preparation of the time of prayer, and provides texts to be used.

Song

Exposition (Procession from place of reservation)

Readings, Homily, Prayers, Songs
(including Liturgy of the Hours) *ad libitum*

Eucharistic Song

Prayer

Reposition (Procession to place of reservation)

Acclamation (which may take the form of a hymn or song to our Lady)

Assisting at a Celebration of the Word
and Communion

The ritual for this form of celebration, approved for use in England and Wales, is *Celebrations of the Word and Communion*. It is available as a download from the website of the Liturgy Office of the Bishops' Conference of England and Wales.[15]

The ritual booklet contains guidance for the preparation and celebration of such services, when they have been approved by the diocesan bishop.

The outline for the rite is as follows:

Introductory Rites

Opening Song

Greeting

Introduction

Penitential Rite

Gloria

Opening Prayer

Liturgy of the Word

Reading

Psalm

Reading

Gospel Acclamation

Gospel

Reflection

Silence

Profession of Faith

General Intercessions

Liturgy of Communion

Transfer of the Blessed Sacrament

The Lord's Prayer

Sign of Peace

Breaking of Bread

Communion

Silence

Thanksgiving

Concluding Rite

Concluding Prayer

Blessing

Dismissal

Italics indicate elements included only on Sundays and Solemnities

The role of Minister of Holy Communion will normally be confined to the Liturgy of Communion. However it is important that this form of celebration, as others, be prepared and ministered collaboratively, and so the ministers will together share in that responsibility.

Commissioning Ministers
of Holy Communion

Two rites are provided here.

The first is the order of Blessing that is commended for use when commissioning ministers for regular service in a community.

The second is provided in the *Roman Missal* for deputing a minister to assist on a single occasion.

Order for the Blessing of commissioned Ministers of Holy Communion[16]

Introduction

1871   It is, first of all, the office of the priest and deacon to minister Holy Communion to the faithful who ask to receive it. It is most fitting, therefore, that they give a suitable part their time to this ministry of their order, depending on the needs of the faithful.

It is the office of an acolyte who has been properly instituted to give communion as an extraordinary minister when the priest and deacon are absent or impeded by sickness, old age, or pastoral ministry or when the number of the faithful at the holy table is so great that the Mass or other service may be unreasonably protracted.

The local Ordinary may give other extraordinary ministers the faculty to give communion whenever it seems necessary for the pastoral benefit of the faithful, and a priest, deacon, or acolyte is not available.

1872 Persons should be authorized to distribute Holy Communion in special circumstances should be commissioned by the local Ordinary or his delegate according to the following rite. The rite should take place in the presence of the people during Mass or outside Mass.

1873 The pastor is the usual minister of his rite. However he may delegate another priest to celebrate it, or a deacon, when it is celebrated outside Mass. The word of God, as proclaimed in the sacred Scripture, lies at the heart of our Christian life and is integral to all our liturgical celebrations.

ORDER OF COMMISSIONING WITHIN MASS

1874 After the gospel reading, the celebrant in the homily, based on the sacred text and pertinent to the particular place and the people involved, explains the meaning of the celebration.

Presentation of the Candidates

1875   *Then he presents to the people those chosen to serve*
       as special ministers, using these or similar words.

Dear friends in Christ, our brothers and sister N. and N. are to be entrusted with administering the Eucharist, with taking Communion to the sick, and with giving it as viaticum to the dying.

The celebrant pauses, and then addresses the candidates.

In this ministry, you must be examples of Christian living in faith and conduct; you must strive to grow in holiness through this sacrament of unity and love. Remember that, though many, we are one body because we share the one bread and one cup.

As ministers of Holy Communion be, therefore, especially observant of the Lord's command to love your neighbour. For when he gave his Body as food to his disciples, he said to them: 'This is my commandment, that you should love one another as I have loved you.'

Examination

1876 *After the address the candidates stand before the*
celebrant, who asks them these questions:

Celebrant:

Are you resolved to undertake the office of giving
the Body and Blood of the Lord to your brothers
and sisters, and so serve to build up the Church?

Candidates: **I am.**

Are you resolved to administer the holy Eucharist
with the utmost care and reverence?

Candidates: **I am.**

Prayer of Blessing

1877 *All stand. The candidates kneel (if possible)*
and the celebrant invites the faithful to pray:

Celebrant:

Dear friends in Christ, let us pray with confidence to
the Father; let us ask him to bestow his blessings on
our brothers and sisters, chosen to be extraordinary
ministers of the Eucharist.

Pause for silent prayer.
The celebrant then continues:

Merciful Father,
creator and guide of your family,
bless ✠ our brothers and sisters N. and N.

May they faithfully give the Bread of life to
your people.

Strengthened by this sacrament,
may they come at last to the banquet of heaven.

We ask this through Christ our Lord.

R. **Amen.**

1878 *Or:*

Gracious Lord,
you nourish us with the Body and Blood
of your Son,
that we might have eternal life.

Bless our brothers and sisters who have been chosen
to give the Bread of heaven and the cup of salvation
to your faithful people.

May the saving mysteries they distribute
lead them to the joys of eternal life.

We ask this through Christ our Lord.

R. **Amen.**

General Intercessions

1879 The general intercessions follow, either in the form
usual at Mass or in the form presented here. The
celebrant concludes the intercessions with the
prayer of blessing. From the following intentions
those best for the occasion may be used or adapted,

or other intentions that apply to the particular circumstances may be composed.

The celebrant says:

The Lord feeds and nourishes us with his life-giving Body and Blood. Let us pray that these ministers of communion be ever faithful to their responsibility of distributing Holy Communion in our community.

R. **Lord, hear our prayer.**

Or:

Hear us, O Lord.

Assisting minister:

For our ministers of communion, that they witness by their deep faith in the Eucharist to the saving mystery of Christ, let us pray to the Lord.

Assisting minister:

For the Church, that the Eucharist we celebrate always be a bond of unity and a sacrament of love for all who partake, let us pray to the Lord.

Assisting minister:

For the sick who will receive holy communion from these ministers, that Christ heal and strengthen them, let us pray to the Lord.

Assisting minister:

For all who are present here, that the Bread of life and cup of salvation we receive at the altar always be our nourishment, let us pray to the Lord.

1880 *The celebrant then says*:

> Lord our God
> teach us to cherish in our hearts
> the paschal mystery of your Son,
> by which you redeemed the world.
>
> Watch over the gifts of grace your love has given us
> and bring them to fulfilment in the glory of heaven.
>
> We ask this through Christ our Lord.
>
> R. **Amen.**

Liturgy of the Eucharist

1881 In the procession of gifts, the newly commissioned ministers carry the vessels with the bread and wine, and at communion may receive the Eucharist under both kinds.

Rite of Deputing a Minister to distribute Holy Communion on a single occasion

1. The Diocesan Bishop has the faculty to permit individual Priests exercising sacred duties to depute a suitable member of the faithful to distribute Holy Communion with them on a single occasion, in cases of real necessity.

2. When one of the faithful is deputed to distribute Communion on a single occasion in such cases, it is

fitting that a mandate to do so should be conferred
according to the following rite.

3. After the Priest Celebrant himself has received the
    Sacrament in the usual way, the extraordinary minister
    comes to the altar and stands before the Celebrant,
    who blesses him or her with these words:

    May the Lord ✠ bless you,
    so that at this Mass you may minister
    the Body and Blood of Christ
    to your brothers and sisters.
    And he or she replies:
    Amen.

4. If the extraordinary minister is to receive the Most
    Holy Eucharist, the Priest gives Communion to the
    minister. Then the Priest gives him or her the ciborium
    or vessel with the hosts or the chalice and together
    they go to administer Communion to the faithful.

Additional resources to support the Ministry of Holy Communion

People's edition of Missal/Lectionary

CTS New Sunday Missal: People's Edition with New Translation of the Mass.

CTS New Daily Missal: People's Edition with New Translation of the Mass (with readings and Mass texts for Weekdays and Sundays).

Universalis - an on-line Missal and Divine Office using the translations approved for use in England and Wales, allowing you access to these books when using Android (including Kindle Fire), iOS (iPhone, iPad and iPod Touch), Mac and Windows. www.universalis.com

General

On the Mass, and the Eucharist

Pope John Paul II (2003) *Ecclesia de Eucharistia*. London, Catholic Truth Society.

Pope John Paul II (2004) *Mane Nobiscum Domine*. London, Catholic Truth Society.

Pope Benedict XVI (2007) *Sacramentum Caritatis*. London, Catholic Truth Society.

Pope Benedict XVI (2010) *Verbum Domini*. London, Catholic Truth Society.

Catholic Bishops' Conferences of England & Wales, Ireland, and Scotland. (1998) *One Bread One Body*. London, Catholic Truth Society.

Catholic Bishops' Conferences of England & Wales. (2005) *Celebrating the Mass*. London, Catholic Truth Society.

Congregation for Divine Worship and Discipline of the Sacraments (2010). *General Instruction of the Roman Missal, 3rd Typical Edition*. London, Catholic Truth Society.

J. D. Crichton (1982) *Christian Celebration: Understanding the Mass* London: Geoffrey Chapman.

Johannes H. Emminghaus (1978): *The Eucharist: Essence, Form, Celebration*. Collegeville, Liturgical Press.

International Committee on English in the Liturgy (2010). *Become One Body One Spirit* (Interactive DVD). Washington, USA, ICEL.

Peter M. J. Stravinskas (2000) *The Bible and the Mass*. Mt Pocono, PA, Newman House Press

Paul Turner (2011) *At the Supper of the Lamb: A Pastoral and Theological Commentary on the Mass*. Chicago, Liturgical Training Publications.

On Scripture

Charpentier, E. (1982) *How to Read the Old Testament*. London, SCM Press.

Charpentier, E. (1982) *How to Read the New Testament*. London, SCM Press.

Pilch, John J (1996-2004) Three series, each of three books, one for each Sunday cycle of the Lectionary. *The Cultural World of the Prophets*; *The Cultural World of the Apostles*; *The Cultural World of Jesus*. Collegeville, Liturgical Press.

Pope Benedict XVI (Ratzinger, J.) (2007) *Jesus of Nazareth*. (3 volumes: *From the Baptism in the Jordan to the Transfiguration; Holy Week: from the Entrance into Jerusalem to the Resurrection; The Infancy Narratives*). London, Bloomsbury, Catholic Truth Society..

Endnotes

[1] The principal guidance with regard to the celebration of Mass is published in the *General Instruction of the Roman Missal* (hereafter GIRM), the introduction to the *Roman Missal* and conveniently published as a separate volume by the Catholic Truth Society (RM12). The Bishops of England and Wales issued a companion pastoral guide, *Celebrating the Mass*, to assist to a greater appreciation and implementation of the *General Instruction*. This was also published by CTS (Do731).

[2] GIRM 91-109.

[3] GIRM 91-109.

[4] For example by the Bishops of England and Wales in *Celebrating the Mass*, 44-46.

[5] It translates the Greek word ανάμνησις (*anamnesis*).

[6] *Directory for Sunday Celebrations in the Absence of a Priest* (Rome 1988), see also Celebrations of the Word and Communion, (Liturgy Office, Bishops Conference of England and Wales, 1996). Both are available on-line at *http://www.liturgyoffice.org.uk/Resources/CWC/index.shtml*

[7] As urged in by Pope Francis in *Evangelii Gaudium*.

[8] Pastoral Letter of Archbishop Vincent Nichols, 28th June 2011 'Receiving Holy Communion'.

[9] Ditto.

[10] *Celebrating the Mass*, 211.

[11] Numbers 6:25.

[12] cf *Celebrating the Mass*, 220, 221.

[13] This will ensure that they also have the rites for the ministering Holy Communion as viaticum, and also where circumstances require, to the rites for the Commendation of the Dying and Prayers for the Dead.

[14] This is to be said, for example in the chapel before visiting those in a hospital ward. It is a moment of prayer that is for the benefit of the minister, rather than for the direct benefit of the communicant.

[15] *http://www.liturgyoffice.org.uk/Resources/CWC/index.shtml*

[16] This Rite comes from the *Book of Blessings* produced for use in the Dioceses of the United States. It is authorised by the Bishops' Conference for England and Wales for interim use in England and Wales.